Dedicated to

Kuldeep Nana Ji.

The Last Call: Air India 182

Amanat Gill

Published by Amanat Gill, 2023.

While every precaution has been taken in the preparation of this book, the publisher assumes no responsibility for errors or omissions, or for damages resulting from the use of the information contained herein.

THE LAST CALL: AIR INDIA 182

First edition. January 11, 2023.

Copyright © 2023 Amanat Gill.

ISBN: 979-8215229750

Written by Amanat Gill.

I miss you dearly

A percentage of funds collected from book sales go into funding resources and education for children in low-income households across my hometown, Moga, Punjab. Thank you for your support.

THE LAST CALL: AIR INDIA 182

Amanat Gill Foundation

"Creating opportunities, one child at a time"

While every precaution has been taken in the preparation of this book, the publisher assumes no responsibility for errors or omissions, or for damages resulting from the use of the information contained herein. All information presented is collected from documentaries, research papers, eye-witnesses (through articles) and other reliable sources..

All rights reserved.

amanats2012@gmail.com

For information about sales promotions and education needs, contact the author directly.

The Last Call

JANUARY 2023

Copyright 2023 AMANAT GILL

Written by Amanat Gill

The Last Call
Air India Flight 182

THE LAST CALL: AIR INDIA 182

AMANAT GILL

PART ONE

THE LAST CALL: AIR INDIA 182

It was not something one could have been prepared for nor was it something anyone involved could have avoided unless they didn't board Flight 182 that day.

Aviation experts at the time were stumped on what could have brought down a jumbo jet that was so popular for its safety record and aerodynamics. Travelers feared taking flights and people questioned the safety of air travel across the globe. Unless answers were found, the aviation industry would be seeing a drop in travelers for months to come as people began to question safety and security not only on the aircraft of Air India but at airports everywhere.

It was a beautiful sunny morning in the Atlantic Ocean on June 23, 1985. The sky was a dusty pink with hints of orange and the sun was just peeking through the horizon.

Just 290 kilometers south of Ireland, flew Air India flight 182 also known as Emperor Kanishka. It was a ginormous Boeing 747 covered in traditional red artistry illustrating the distinct designs of India and its culture.

Air India had transformed their aircraft with traditional artwork around the windows and doors. It was an attempt to stand out from the rest and a way to bring a little bit of India everywhere their fleet visited. The designs were said to represent warmth, a welcoming atmosphere, and incomparable hospitality. India is undoubtedly a very hospitable nation with flavorful cuisine, friendly people and so many cultures, so it made sense for the airline to design in such a way.

It's 8:06 am on that June 23rd morning and First Officer Satwant Bhinder makes radio contact with Irish air traffic control. He's an experienced Captain with many flying hours, but today he's acting as First Officer on this flight while Captain Narendra takes control. "Air India one eight two, good morning!"

"Go ahead please." Michael Quinn, the air traffic controller on duty at Shannon International Airport, replied.

"Air India one eight two is five one north, one five west at flight level three one zero."

"Air India one eight two, roger, cleared for landing. Flight level three one zero."

"Air India one eight two, maintain flight level three one zero, clear to land in London."

An average exchange between the first officer and air traffic controller had just confirmed the aircraft had no restrictions to make a landing at their second stopover, Heathrow International Airport.

The flight's journey started several hours ago in Canada. Passengers had connected from various places, mainly from a CP Air flight, originating in Vancouver. The plane had gone through Montreal, and was on its way to its second layover in Heathrow, before making it home to Delhi.

It was the last week of June, meaning schools were finishing and many children were going back home to visit family and friends. Accompanying them would be parents and other guardians. In total, 307 passengers and 22 crew members were on board that day.

Shortly, the plane would start its descent as First Officer Bhinder and Captain Narendra would start their landing checklist. But that never happens.

Moments later, Michael and his co-worker Thomas Lane notice a rather strange sight. It was a quiet morning at the

THE LAST CALL: AIR INDIA 182

control center and their radar only had 3 flights, however, they had all seemed to merge together, making it impossible to read the flight levels and other vital flight details.

Computers and radars have a long way to go for development at this point in history, therefore seeing systems get overwhelmed, reset or shut down from time to time, isn't all that uncommon, especially when you have three aircraft traveling in one direction, parallel.

Air India 182 is heading west at 31,000 feet, while on top at 35,000 feet a TWA jet and at 37,000 feet a CP flight. International aviation rules allowed aircraft to travel in the same direction as long as at least 1000 feet were left above and beneath for safety reasons.

Having not-so-advanced technology, the computers at the air traffic control center were overwhelmed with the information they received all at once. As the aircraft is being reset on the screen, two of them reappear in seconds, but Air India is nowhere to be seen.

"I don't have Air India." Michael turned to Thomas. Both exchange a look of unease.

"Air India do you read?" Quinn questions.

Silence.

"Air India one eight two, this is Shannon Air Control, do you read?"

Nothing.

It's 8:14 am and Michael proceeds to pick up the phone and make a distress call to Search and Rescue. It was an impulsive call. Something pushed Michael that day to make that distress call within one minute of the aircraft disappearing, even though standards stated distress calls should be ideally made 20 minutes after no contact with the aircraft.

Ships and helicopters are sent out to the aircraft's last location within minutes of Michael's call. More than 200 kilometers south of Cork, Ireland, a search is underway for a missing jumbo jet.

2 hours have gone by when a Canadian-owned cargo ship in the radius responds to the distress call. They had found a piece of what looked like an aircraft in the freezing waters of the Atlantic. A design, red in color could be seen on the metal piece, which almost looked like Air India's unique design. It was.

It was a side piece of the aircraft found floating in the middle of the water. What had happened to the rest of the aircraft? What had happened to the passengers?

It didn't take long for the news to circulate across the world about an Air India airplane going down in the Atlantic. Families of the passengers back in Canada and the ones awaiting in India are in a state of horror. They are praying their loved ones have survived and that a minor mishap on the aircraft caused the window panel to fall out. However, this isn't the case.

Search and Rescue start pulling out more broken pieces of the airplane. Luggage bags, seats, and all kinds of parts and pieces from the aircraft are pulled out from the ocean in the next several hours. Along with those pieces are pulled the dead bodies of the 180 passengers and crew. It was obvious, no one survived.

It was news that no one was prepared to receive. No one had hoped to receive it. The passengers had boarded the flight with excitement to visit home, yet they never made it. You can only imagine, your loved one boarding a flight and waving goodbye at the airport, promising to call you once they reach Delhi, and a couple of hours later you find out from the news, their plane has

THE LAST CALL: AIR INDIA 182

crashed into the ocean.

One can't be prepared to receive such news. Sadness, anger, and a storm of emotions flood your heart. Though you hope for good news, deep down you know there are no survivors. That's exactly how families felt when this information circulated around the globe.

Investigators had made it to the dock where pieces of the airplane and dead bodies were being brought throughout the day. Investigators would need to find answers fast to avoid another catastrophic accident, that is if faulty parts or equipment were to blame.

While this was taking place in one corner of the world, in another, a bomb had gone off in a terminal at Narita Airport, Japan. It had taken two lives and injured five. The world was confused as to what was happening today. First, an aircraft goes missing, then a bomb goes off at an airport terminal. Link? Both stories originated in Canada.

As the bodies are beginning to go through autopsies, investigators hope to find some sort of clues that would indicate what had happened on board. For now, they would have to rely on the information they had from the black and red boxes of the plane.

The black and red boxes are the flight data recorder and flight voice recorder. The flight data recorder records any and all settings that the plane has or is being changed to. For example, the autopilot is turned off at what time would be recorded in this box. The flight voice recorder records any and all conversations happening in the cockpit at all times. These boxes were designed in 1942 by Finnish engineer, Veijo Hietala to maximize safety, but as commercial airlines adapted these instruments, it was proving to be quite helpful during the investigations as aircraft accidents were analyzed with precision.

For example, during the 1980s there were many aircraft accidents and incidents due to aircraft still being engineered to be flawless and technology still advancing. Some accidents that occurred before 1985 were solved with heavy aid from the black and red boxes, as they provided insight into what was happening in the cockpit. It could be something as little as a small setting a pilot forgot to change that could bring down a plane. Therefore, it was easier to pick this up with the data recorder than it was to assume what happened or rely on pilot interviews, that is if they had survived.

Luckily, the flight data and voice recorders had been designed to withstand a large amount of force and to survive underwater for up to 30 days while sending communication signals above sea level, so investigators would find them. In this case, where the plane came down in the Atlantic was a large area to cover and the weather forecast of that day has drastically changed to rain and heavy winds, causing larger waves that would move the wreckage faster than it could be recovered.

The wreckage of the plane was taken to an empty hangar so investigators could lay it out and examine each piece in detail, while the 180 recovered dead bodies were taken to a local autopsy center to be analyzed. Pieces of the plane were hardly intact. There were several small pieces found and maybe a few large pieces. It was obvious, some sort of intense impact had brought this plane down, but what?

Decompression? Substantial drag? Explosives? Pilot Suicide? There were so many possibilities running through the investigators' minds, yet hardly any evidence to support any of

THE LAST CALL: AIR INDIA 182

the theories.

Decompression is a loss of cabin pressure in the airplane and can present itself in three levels of intensity. Cabin Safety.com gets into detail about the levels.

First is insidious decompression, The intensity is low and signs may not present themselves right away and passengers may feel its impact slowly. Usually, oxygen masks drop and passengers may become hypoxic.

Fast forward to 2005, Helios Flight 522 is a classic example of insidious decompression in addition to pilot error. During the flight's climb to cruising altitude, the pilots did not set the cabin pressure to its required setting, which over time resulted in the loss of cabin pressure. Slowly, all passengers and crew began to lose consciousness and did not survive, as the plane ran out of fuel and crashed into a hillside in Greece.

Oxygen masks had dropped to aid the passengers and crew, however, later investigations revealed there was no contact with air traffic from Helios to request a lower flight level - indicating oxygen masks not working or running out and not providing enough time for the pilots to regain consciousness and bring the plane down to a safer altitude. Oxygen masks at the time were able to provide breathable air for about 12 minutes, which would be an appropriate amount of time for pilots to get their aircraft down to a lower altitude where cabin pressure would be tolerable.

Second comes rapid decompression, which comes with the traditional hypoxia, however, it's more obvious as there can be structural damage to the aircraft and loose items will fly, cabin air will rush towards the damaged area, and a nose dive descent occurs.

Southwest Airlines Flight 812 in 2011 suffered metal fatigue which caused a hole to rupture in its fuselage (body of the plane). This happened during the flight as the plane was making its way to its cruising altitude of 36000 feet. The ruptured hole caused rapid decompression however, oxygen masks were dropped in time and only two people suffered minor injuries.

Lastly, the most impactful type of decompression is explosive decompression. This occurs when there's a large explosion that causes damage to the structure of the aircraft. Oxygen masks drop, loose articles will fly out along with all the cabin air and a severe nose dive descent will begin.

Aloha Airlines Flight 243 experienced explosive damage to its aircraft in 1988 which caused one passenger to fly out of the aircraft. Metal fatigue and poor maintenance had been the cause behind the explosion, but thankfully the plane landed with half of its roof ripped off. It was no less than a miracle.

Theory 1 of decompression was being explored for Air India 182. There were pictures being analyzed of the crash sight. The pattern that the wreckage was lying in illustrated an important clue. The wreckage in the ocean was sitting in a circular pattern, instead of a linear one. A linear pattern of wreckage would have suggested that the aircraft had hit the water and then broke apart, leaving a large part of the fuselage intact. The latter would suggest the aircraft falling apart before hitting the ocean. It was obvious from these pictures that the plane had gone through damage before hitting the Atlantic, so whatever happened must have happened in the air.

It was quite possible that a form of decompression, mostly rapid or explosive, had occurred on board, but evidence would be needed to support this theory. Investigators now sat down to

THE LAST CALL: AIR INDIA 182

listen and analyze the black and red boxes and to pick up any clues that would suggest a decompression in the cabin of flight 182.

Investigators sat around the black box, the flight data recorder, and had hoped they would find some sort of clue suggesting a faulty setting that could have caused depressurization in the cabin. After multiple listens, rewinding, and pausing, there was nothing that could have suggested the plane's systems had failed at some point. The 737 was flying with all the right settings and the pilots had it under control at all times. There were no alarms going off in the cockpit to warn the pilots of a possible faulty setting, nor was there any conversation between the pilots suggesting they were trying to solve an issue. There was no record of the oxygen masks dropping on the data recorder either.

As this possibility is being explored, maintenance records of the airplane make it to the investigators. The 737 has had its routine checkups done regularly and has passed them with flying colors, but on this leg of the flight, there was one difference spotted in the structure of the plane.

Most 737s come with the standard four engines along with the ability to fly on two if the other two are to fail during flight. Though all engines were working and the hydraulics were flowing and there was enough fuel, there was one engine that could've presented itself as a potential hazard.

Flight 182 was flying with 5 engines. It was an extra engine that was not in operation during the flight. It had received some repairs and was being transported to India with this flight. Could this extra engine have created some sort of substantial drag that eventually brought down the whole airplane?

Substantial drag, which can also be called aerodynamic drag, is a force that goes against the motion of the object. To simplify, here's an illustration. When an airplane makes its landing, the ailerons on the wings are lifted upwards so the motion of air flowing on the wing of the plane changes, which eventually helps bring the plane to a stop. When taking off, these ailerons are put down so the wing's surface is smooth as possible and the air flowing on the wind during take-off creates as much lift as possible.

A classic example of the importance of airflow on an aircraft can be dated to 1992. USAir Flight 405 came crashing into Flushing Bay after two takeoffs had failed. The aircraft's wings had not been de-iced properly before takeoff, resulting in an interruption in the airflow. As the plane climbed, the interruption in airflow caused an aerodynamic stall which then caused the pilots to lose control of the aircraft and eventually ended in pieces in the icy waters just a few miles off from La Guardia Airport.

Obviously, in Air India 182's case, the weather was not an important factor, as the plane had traveled from Toronto, where in the middle of June, temperatures could reach the higher 30s. The extra engine was suspected of creating substantial drag.

The extra engine wouldn't have put the aircraft in a nose dive, however. The weight of the extra engine would have required maybe a faster airspeed. Maybe more fuel on the opposite side to balance the weight? Reports indicated that fuel levels were appropriate, pilots were aware of the extra engines, and had taken all the right precautions to transport the engine safely.

If substantial drag was the reason behind the plane going down, wouldn't the wreckage be laying in a linear pattern?

Substantial drag bringing an aircraft down would slowly drag the plane towards the ocean instead of bringing it crashing and then smashing into the waters. The wreckage laying in a circular pattern did not support the theory of aerodynamic drag, so investigators were back to square one.

If the data in the airplane was correct then maybe the voice recorders could provide some sort of clues as to what happened. As investigators listened, only normal day-to-day conversation could be heard. The last thing to be recorded was the exchange with Michael Quinn in Ireland, then a short couple of seconds of silence, a muffled noise, and then complete silence. There was nothing after that.

What had caused the boxes to stop recording immediately? It was definite that there was a decompression on board, but something had to cause it. The recovered plane pieces indicated the fuselage breaking a part, but the plane's structure didn't have any signs of stress, nor did the pieces indicate faulty mechanisms and poor maintenance.

The search for answers was underway and the autopsies had finally revealed that the passengers whose bodies were recovered had all died before hitting the water, except two. Upon investigation, it was concluded that the two passengers that died with water filling into their lungs, died due to drowning, but were also seated at the back of the plane. The rest of the passengers who died before impact, were all sitting near the front or middle of the aircraft.

Whatever decompression happened, happened near the front, which resulted in the plane breaking into several pieces.

The last test that investigators could possibly turn to was an explosives test. Though everyone wanted this to come back negative the opposite happened. Explosives debris had been found on this aircraft's broken pieces. Specifically, material that can be used to construct bombs.

A bomb explosion would perfectly explain the impact of the decompression, passengers' deaths before hitting the water, the intensity of the damage, and why the data and voice recorders had stopped even though they were designed to tolerate heavy amounts of damage.

How would this bomb have gotten on the airplane? Who was responsible for this? Though these questions flooded everyone's minds, there was already a suspicion about who was involved.

PART TWO

Since the 1600s the British had been trading with India for their silk, cotton, rare spices, and tea that could not be found anywhere around the world. During this time, while they traded, the British had been successful in taking over small parts of India, and after 157 years of doing so, Britain had control over large areas of India.

Winning the Battle of Plassey in 1757 let the British fully rule part of the country. The battle was between the British East and French East company. However, there was still a large chunk of the country that the Mughals had control over that was demolished a little while later by the British, but even after that, they did not have Punjab and Bengal under their rule.

In the 1900s, Queen Victoria claimed to make her Indian subjects better by teaching them British ways of thinking and eliminating cultural practices that were not necessary according to her. This also led to a very unethical concept of Divide and Rule. This practice would instigate the Hindus and Muslims against each other as it focused on taking religion and turning people against each other. This would later prove to be a devastating concept that would not only separate a country but separate hearts, families, and lives.

By 1849 the British had taken over the state of Punjab, making it the last to be ruled, for only 98 years while most of India was ruled for 100 years.

The British suspected Indians to be disloyal towards them despite their fight against Germany in World War I, so in 1919, the Rowlatt Act had been passed. This Act allowed the government to prison suspected insurgents without trial or questioning which led to the arrest of two important political figures who were connected to Mahatma Gandhi. This led to a public outcry in the nation.

At the Jallianwala Bagh Gardens, Amritsar, General Dyer, representing the British, thought the Indians that were rioting, were initiating violence, which led him to order Gurkha soldiers and Iranians to fight the Sikhs. They blocked all exits of the garden and streets and fired without any communication. The protesters were unarmed and unaware of their fate, which resulted in 1000 deaths, even though the British tried to sell 357. This was known as the Amritsar Massacre.

In 1942, the British sent Labor Politician Stafford Cripps to India with the offer of future dominion status in return for recruiting more soldiers for World War II. It was also said at this time Cripps had made a secret agreement with Muslims living in India with an offer that allowed them to opt-out of a future Indian State.

At this point, Gandhi, who led all the freedom movements and the Indian National Congress, did not agree to the offer and started 'Quit India', a movement that demanded the British to leave India. This led the British to arrest Gandhi and his wife and other leaders of the National Congress.

The arrest upset a lot of Gandhi's followers therefore, people created mass demonstrations all over British India and this time the British could not stop anyone.

It was also too late to stop the Hindus and Muslims from fighting. The Divide and Rule policy had created hatred between the two and the way Muslims were instigated against Hindus by the British had turned this environment in British India violent. Riots broke out and there was chaos all over the country. Amidst this chaos, Hindus, Muslims, and Sikhs now had decided to divide the country. People fled both ways of the border and on

August 14th, 1947, Pakistan was an independent nation, and the following day, India was too.

Yes, there would be no risk of fights breaking out every day caused by religious differences, but there were families that would never see each other again. There were people who would never know if their loved ones survived or not. Since that day, there have been two countries on any map you see, separated by a border, and political and religious system all thanks to the British. A line on a map however will never separate the people that once called each other brothers and sisters.

Earlier that same year, on February 12th, 1947 in Rode, Punjab, Joginder Singh, and Nihal Kaur gave birth to their seventh son, Jarnail Singh Brar. His six brothers were identified as Jagir Singh, Jagjit Singh, Jugraj Singh, Harjeet Singh, Veer Singh, and Harcharan Singh. He had a sister named Manjeet Kaur as well.

Everyone in this family was a devotee of the Sikh religion and Gurus. They had all gone through the sacred Amrit ceremony of Khalsa, initiated by the tenth Sikh Guru, Guru Gobind Singh Ji.

The rules of Khalsa after the Amrit ceremony include not removing hair from any part of the body, not using tobacco, alcohol, or other intoxicants, one shall not eat meat that has been slaughtered off of an animal, and finally wear the initiated physical symbols of Khalsa, which include: Kanga (comb), Kachera (underpants), Kirpan, Kada (metal bracelet) and kesh (a head full of hair).

As Jarnail grew up in such a devoted family, it was obvious that he too went through the Amrit Ceremony. He did so at the age of five.

At a young age, his family started teaching him the prayers of the Guru Granth Saab which can also be addressed as the Holy Scripture of Sikhism. He attended school like his brothers and took up farming until 1964. He married Pritam Kaur later in his life who gave him two sons.

Farming did not become Singh's career for long. He had a larger-than-life purpose.

The Damdami Taksal was a traveling university that promoted the education of the Sikh religion and Gurus to young children. It was founded by Guru Gobind Singh Ji and the first leader was Shaheed Baba Deep Singh Ji. Sant Gurbachan Singh Khalsa Bhindranwale was the 12th leader serving at the time he interacted with Jarnail Singh.

Young Jarnail stood out to Gurbachan Singh Khalsa due to his devotion and passion for Sikhism. Jarnail Singh, for the year to come, took up a course about Sikh history, spirituality, and ideologies that were left by the ten Sikh Gurus:

Guru Nanak Dev Ji founded Sikhism and would travel far and wide to educate people about Sikhism. Guru Ji composed 974 hymns for the Guru Granth Sahib Ji as well.

Guru Angad Dev Ji took over the responsibility to lead the Sikh tradition after Guru Nanak Dev Ji's death and is known for formalizing the Gurmukhi alphabet.

Guru Amar Das Ji wrote and put together hymns for the Adi Granth and set the rituals relating to child-naming, marriage, funerals, and for celebrations such as Maghi, Diwali, and Vaisakhi.

Guru Ram Das Ji founded the city of Amritsar in 1547 which was previously known as Ramdaspur. Also responsible for creating the design of the Golden Temple.

Guru Arjan Dev Ji built the Golden Temple and completed the Adi Granth and placed it in the Temple and was the creator of the Sukhmani Sahib hymn. Cities such as Taran Taran Sahib and Kartarpur, Jalandhar were also founded by Guru Ji. Guru Arjan Dev Ji was executed by the Mughal Emperor for not changing his religion.

Guru Hargobind Singh Ji gave Sikhism their military character and constructed the Akal Takht as a sign of political independence.

Guru Har Rai Ji maintained a large army of Sikh soldiers and excommunicated his eldest son for changing the Adi Granth verse to the liking of Aurangzeb.

Guru Harkrishan Sahib Ji was the youngest Guru Ji and succeeded his father, Guru Har Rai Ji. Guru Ji had the shortest reign at just over two years.

Guru Tegh Bahadur Ji was publicly beheaded for not converting to Islam and composed 116 hymns in the Guru Granth Sahib.

Guru Gobind Singh Ji was responsible for founding Khalsa and its five sacred symbols. Guru Ji's sons were executed by the Mughals and buried alive in walls.

Kartar Singh Khalsa, the successor of Gurbachan Singh Khalsa had a lot to say about young Jarnail when he was in school. "…He is a bright student with a bright future." And he also said that Jarnail wasn't like any other student.

He would recite prayers more than the others and if anyone spoke against his religion, he would stop associating with that person for good. Jarnail Singh had been noted from the beginning as a very dominant personality. He possessed the quality of a powerful leader before even becoming one.

One awful afternoon, Kartar Singh's life came to an end due to a fatal car accident. He saw Jarnail as the future of the Taksal so he appointed him as the new leader before passing away. Jarnail Singh Brar was sworn in on August 25th, 1977 at the Damdami Taksal as Jarnail Singh Bhindranwale.

It didn't take Jarnail Singh much time to become a great leader. At that time Bhindranwale had two bright visions which he and his partners thought could make Punjab a better place to be.

The first was he wanted all the Sikhs in Punjab to go back to their roots. He wanted everyone to follow the rules of Khalsa and get as many people as he could to go through the Amrit ceremony. He wanted everyone to quit wrongdoings such as the use of alcohol, drugs, and prostitution. He saw a vision of everyone being pure which would make them mentally and physically healthier. It would set Punjab up for a brighter future.

To do so, Bhindranwale would visit cities and villages near and far. His goal on this journey was to inform the maximum number of people why going through the Amrit ceremony was beneficial. He would use the sacrifices made by the ten Sikh Gurus as examples to inspire the people of Punjab.

The second goal for Bhindranwale was for Sikhs to be recognized as a majority instead of a minority in India. In 1947, upon independence from the British, Nehru and Gandhi were appointed as the leaders of the New Nation.

Sikhs were promised full rights in India and no bill would be passed without their consent. The New Nation leaders feared that if Punjab went back to being independent like they were before being taken over by the British, India would struggle. After all, wheat and rice growth were big in the Punjab region. They wanted to keep Sikhs part of the new country and to do this they made promises;

"...in future, the Congress shall accept no constitution which does not meet with the satisfaction of the Sikhs"

There were several claims specifically made by Nehru that convinced Sikhs that India would be a prosperous place for them, but it seemed that Nehru soon forgot his promises.

In 1956, India reorganized its states based on languages but left Punjab out and did not recognize Punjabi as one of India's national languages, and denied recognition of the Sikhs in the Constitution Act of India. When Nehru was reminded of his promises, he replied "...circumstances have now changed."

Nehru wanted to keep Sikhs in India. Therefore, Sikhs were and are always denied any demands they put forth. Were they a threat? Seems like it because, for example, a lot of gross domestic product comes from agriculture in the state of Punjab even though they only made up 2% of the population at the time. Nehru did not want to lose these resources. In order to be treated fairly in India, Bhindranwale and company put forth a resolution.

This act took place in 1973 known as the Anandpur Sahib Resolution. This resolution was made up of 12 religious and political requests to the Indian government. Sikhs wanted a separate identity from the Hindus because their religion, beliefs, values, and attitudes differed greatly. The resolution included regional autonomy, the return of the stolen city; Chandigarh, special status in the union, the return of areas that spoke Punjabi to the state of Punjab, a fair share of electricity, stopping the

THE LAST CALL: AIR INDIA 182

unfair distribution of Punjab's water into neighboring states, return of administration of the Punjab Electric Board and a few more.

To Bhindranwale and company, it did seem most of these requests were reasonable. The government thought otherwise and argued not all of them could be met as giving back such powers would be a difficult task.

Bhindranwale and company initially told the Indian government if the Anandpur Sahib Resolution was accepted reasonably they would continue to live with India in peace. If these could not be met then the demand for Khalistan would grow and Bhindranwale would not stop this.

Bhindranwale never adamantly demanded Khalistan, he would just support it if it came to be, as he had stated in his rallies. The government's decision was to deny this resolution because it would divide the country once more. For example, the water that Punjab wanted back did go through other states as well and it didn't make sense to the government so they stated it was not fair to snatch the water and give it to one state, they rather keep it flowing. In reality, the distribution of water situation is a bit complicated.

At this point, it is vital to mention that in the year 1975 Indira Gandhi was found guilty of election fraud. Allahabad High Court found Mrs. Gandhi guilty of misusing government machinery in the election campaigns.

Yes, she was known as one of the most powerful Prime Ministers, yet this power came from wrongdoing. Her response to this was to suspend the constitution so she could stay in office. From that day to January 1977, India was under a state of 'Emergency' which was formally issued by President Fakhruddin

Ali Ahmed. This allowed Gandhi to use a political tactic called Rule by Decree, resulting in her resignation as the PM being unnecessary. Rule by Decree in simpler words enables the Prime Minister to rule the country under any circumstance without internal or external pressures and they cannot be thrown out of office during the time period.

These events led Sikhs to a peaceful protest demanding Indira be held liable for her wrongdoing. It did not matter if she was the Prime minister, if she did wrong, justice had to be served. This protest resulted in 50,000 Sikhs going to jail for creating a so-called chaotic environment. Even today in India, if a common man is found guilty, he can spend his entire life in jail without a hearing yet for any political figure, the law changes in a blink of an eye.

A few months later in early 1978, the Nirankari Sant organized a convention with permission from the government to celebrate the birth of Khalsa. The views of the Nirankaris differed from Bhindranwale which caused a big problem.

Nirankaris believe themselves to be a part of the Sikh religion however they believe the Holy Scripture of Sikhism is an open book that can be added to by generations to come and refuse to recognize God with any image. Bhindranwale strongly opposed these beliefs and acted against them during this convention.

You could see it in Bhindranwale's eyes. The passion for his community and the fierce rage for anyone against it. His blood boiled at anyone speaking against Khalsa. Bhindranwale had one image of Khalsa in his mind, that had been passed on for generations. He was not able to bear the challenge of this different perspective.

Bhindranwale and allies barged into the convention and shot several Nirankaris. During this violence, two of Bhindranwale's men were shot and eleven were, from the opposition. Bhindranwale's close ally, Fauja Singh tried firing at the leader of the Nirankaris; Gurbachan Singh but was shot by his bodyguard. Seeing this, Bhindranwale fled the convention and came into the limelight with international media.

Bhindranwale had become so aggressive with his approach by now that whoever spoke against his views on the Sikh religion didn't live long. While he studied at the Taksal even Kartar Singh used to note how Bhindranwale was a special child. His passion to get justice created a human that would not listen to anything against his religion.

Gurbachan Singh's murder led the police to suspect Bhindranwale, even though he wasn't the one to physically shoot him. Jarnail and their allies then decided to shelter in the Golden Temple because the police could not inflame their religious sentiments inside the holy place.

The Golden Temple also addressed as the Darbar Saab or Harmandir Saab, was founded in the year 1547 and was designed by the fourth Sikh guru, Guru Ramdas Singh Ji. Guru Arjun Dev Ji built it and completed the Adi Granth (Holy Scripture of Sikhism) and placed it in the Gurdwara. It is in the city of Amritsar, Punjab, India.

At this time, it is said that Bhindranwale's allies hid ammunition and guns inside the Golden Temple complex.

In 1981, Lala Jagat Narain, editor and founder of the newspaper, Punjab Kesari, also a strong supporter of the Nirankari movement, was found dead. Due to him writing against Bhindranwale's movement, the police again thought

Bhindranwale was behind this murder and issued a warrant for his arrest.

Bhindranwale did give himself up in September 1981 but his followers freed him. Upon Jarnail's arrest, his followers initiated violence around the state which included hijacking buses, derailing trains, and attacking people.

An Air India flight with 111 passengers and 8 crew traveling from Srinagar to Delhi was hijacked at knife point. They rerouted the plane and landed in Lahore, Pakistan. The hijackers confronted Natwar Singh, India's ambassador in Pakistan to accept their demands.

Jarnail Singh Bhindranwale was released in October of the year due to a lack of evidence in the murder.

With all the violence brewing in the country, it was getting dangerous for Bhindranwale to be out on the streets without protection from potential arrests coming his way. In 1982, the head of Shiromani Akali Dal, Harchand Singh Longowal invited Bhindranwale and his 200-armed allies to make the Golden Temple their headquarters permanently to avoid arrest.

Founded on December 14th, 1920, the Shiromani Akali Dal is a Sikhism political party in India. This party's goal is to give Sikh's a voice to their views, and they believe politics and religion go hand in hand.

Many Sikhs decided to leave the country due to this unrest. Some took their families to Canada and America while others went to Europe. Inderjit Singh had departed India at this moment.

Throughout the months to come the violence did not stop. There was chaos everywhere with murders happening all over the state. Bhindranwale's company responsible for these murders would use local Gurudwaras as hideouts because the police were not able to make any arrests inside a temple.

Shiromani's leader, Longowal had now joined hands with the Congress and called Bhindranwale out for his acts. However, the Indian government had confirmed they would not confront anyone inside a Gurudwara due to potentially hurting Sikh sentiments.

Now, people were getting away with wrongdoings and using these temples as a place to not face justice. So at this point, the Parliament of India had come to an agreement to arrest Bhindranwale due to him supporting and being a part of such a violent environment in the state. Bhindranwale, knowing his arrest was not far, then convinced president Tohra of the Supreme Gurudwara Parbandhak Committee (SGPC), to shift his headquarters to the Akal Takht.

The SGPC is responsible for the management of Gurudwaras in Punjab, Himachal Pradesh, and Chandigarh.

Bhindranwale was granted permission by Tohra but not the head priest of the temple because the head priest abided by the fact that the Akal Takht was never to be taken over by anyone but the founding Gurus. Bhindranwale had no other choice but to avoid this arrest and so he had to stay put in the Akal Takht.

The Akal Takht was constructed by the sixth Sikh Guru named Shiri Guru Hargobind Singh Ji as a sign of political sovereignty. It is a place of justice and a place of consideration of temporal issues. It means 'The Throne of the Timeless One" and is one of the five seats of power in the Akali Dal. It is located right across from the Golden Temple.

From the years 1981 to late 1983, Sikhs that were even peacefully protesting for their rights were arrested without warrants. Some Sikhs had the poor fate of being arrested and tortured without any participation in the protests. This also included 250 Sikhs being killed in fake encounters by the police. It is a familiar argument that is still used in Indian courts today.

By December 1983, Bhindranwale and his allies had made the Golden Temple complex a place stored with armory and headquarters of extremist activities. One of the people to speak against this was the former leader of the Akal Takht. Eighty-year-old Giani Partap Singh, was also found murdered in his home later that month.

Others that spoke against Bhindranwale or the movement for Khalistan were also reported dead, and this time everyone knew who was behind these actions. The movement to make Punjab better again was on a journey that was doing the complete opposite.

Up until now, it was a goal with pure intentions started by a passionate young man. Now it had turned into something ugly that might separate the country again and even separate the people. Why was this violence necessary? Why were those innocent deaths necessary? We have a leader who believed in Khalsa strongly and abided by every rule in the Guru Granth Sahib, yet it was okay for him to use violence to accomplish his goals.

In the months leading up to June 1984, violence increased across the state and fear grew. Bhindranwale's militants had killed several people by shooting, hijacking buses, setting vehicles on fire, bank robberies, and railway station arson. The government's people were also mixed in which made it hard to tell whose side was fighting who. It now seemed like we had lost the Bhindranwale we started out with. Who was this violent man? The Indian government had to stop him before a civil war would break out.

Around January 1984, the Indian government decided to negotiate with Bhindranwale before taking any further actions which involved not only the Golden Temple but Sikh sentiments.

The government tried peaceful negotiations, tried asking the Akalis for help, and lastly asked President Tohra. Not a single effort had worked. Bhindranwale was adamant about his argument and now was in nobody's control. Jarnail Singh was faced with the abandoning of Longowal from his side and the entire government system against him. It was also mentioned in some places that Longowal and Tohra both had left Bhindranwale's side as June 1984 neared.

Bhindranwale stated that "...this bird is alone" claiming that he could fight by himself because in the end "Sikhs can neither live in India nor with India...the country was not fair to his people".

During this battle, the Golden Temple, a holy place where people go to pray, had seen the worst. The complex was being filled with weapons that were being smuggled in by the religious service trucks entering the complex daily. After his dismissal from the army, General Shabeg Singh joined Bhindranwale's army. Shabeg Singh had been spiritually touched upon his first meeting with Jarnail Singh which led him to join his tribe.

The Akal Takht had been allegedly disfigured and weapons were placed in a predetermined formation, ready for a battle at any time. Machine guns and riffles were the common weaponry found. There were holes drilled into the Akal Takht walls for guns to fit through. There were walls smashed to create passageways from the basements to the Takht from all sides. Sandbags bordered the Takht for protection and new brick walls followed. Every building in the complex had been prepared similarly for a potential battle excluding the Golden Temple.

Kuldip Singh Brar, Lt. General of the Indian Army was given orders from the government to capture this misguided man and his militants. This project was code-named *Operation Blue Star* with two subcategories. *Operation Metal* led by Brar was focused on the Golden Temple and complex while *Operation Shop* was to capture militants in the countryside and other temples in the state. The only people not deserving to be in this situation were the pilgrims.

From Bhindranwale's side, Jarnail Singh himself, Shabeg Singh, and Amrik Singh (president of All India Sikh Students Federation) were ready for the first gunfire while the Indian military had General Krishnaswamy and Lt. Kuldip Singh Brar waiting.

June 2nd was when international exits through Kashmir were blocked and troops were stationed all over Punjab. The military had also begun to take control of Amritsar and prepared themselves. An officer was sent in as a pilgrim to note how the defense was prepared. As night fell, traveling was banned into and out of the state, and water and electricity were cut off. All forms of communication and media coverage were banned as well.

June 3rd: The curfew had been lifted as this day in history celebrates the martyrdom of Guru Arjan Dev Ji. This allowed many pilgrims to enter the complex but 200-Sikh militants were successful in escaping as well. The curfew came into action again as night fell and this time Brar's team had blocked all exits to the temple and were surrounding it from each side. It is important to note what Kuldip Brar, a Sikh himself, said before the battle began: "This action is not against Sikhs or the Sikh religion. It is against terrorism."

June 4th: The day was filled with announcements from the military on loudspeakers asking Bhindranwale to peacefully surrender. Upon this refusal, the military destroyed the outer defenses. The army brought in tanks on the roads outside the complex and helicopters above. The former leader of the SGPC, Tohra was sent in to negotiate once again but upon his failure to do so, there was no improvement.

June 5th: Sources note that around 40-72 other Gurudwaras in the state were attacked. The military had planned to start firing from the front and two sides at the Golden Temple complex to secure the northern wing. After two failed attempts, the military was able to take control in the Darshani Deori which was right across the Akal Takht. The military tried using bombs, but they backfired and when entering the south side there was heavy firing from the Langar rooftop. There was a heavy door on the south side that needed to be opened. Since it took a long time, many casualties occurred on the military side. At this time three tanks entered the complex. No matter where the military tried to take control, Bhindranwale's side was ahead and the military experienced more casualties.

June 6th: The tanks were given a thumbs up to fire at the Akal Takht. After this firing took place, the Akal Takht was fully damaged, and the firing had significantly decreased.

June 7th: The day the Indian military got into the Akal Takht and found the dead bodies of Bhindranwale, Shabeg Singh, and Amrik Singh. They now almost had full control over the Golden Temple complex.

June 10th: Up until the night of June 9, there was a bit more firing back and forth from underground but by June 10th Operation Blue Star had come to an end.

Shortly after the Operation had ended all of India heard the news about Jarnail Singh's death. Some were quite happy to hear this while others and their hopes were completely shattered. People and their riots had settled down and the arguments were over. Curfews had been lifted and all operations in the state of Punjab had resumed. In an interview, Kuldip Singh Brar explained why things were done in that manner. "We couldn't wait any longer and the task had to be done for the army's safety."

To many people, Jarnail was a saint but to Brar, he was something else. "...he might have started out as a saint, but he didn't end like one, let me tell you that." He said later on in a television interview.

Days after the operation had ended, President Zail Singh made a visit to the complex but was shot from a neighboring building. Chief of Army Staff, Arun Shridhar Vaidya was assassinated in 1986 in Pune by two Sikhs.

In the eighteenth-century Ahmad Shah Abdali attacked the Golden Temple and died after 157 days. The Temple was constructed again by Maharaja Ranjit Singh; he also secured the upper level of the Temple with pure gold to avoid destruction again. After Gandhi ordered attacks, she also was put into a similar situation.

The Akal Takht, after Blue star, was built again but was named Sarkar Takht to indicate it was a government project, but many people after that took over and built it themselves, and the name changed back to the Akal Takht.

THE LAST CALL: AIR INDIA 182

On the other hand, Indira Gandhi was informed by her personnel that she should change the duty of her Sikh bodyguards because they might seek revenge after being disturbed by the 1984 events.

Gandhi kept the two bodyguards where they were, but she didn't know that she made the biggest mistake of her life by doing that. Two of her bodyguards were planning her assassination.

Beant Singh, a Sikh personal bodyguard of Indira had gone to the Golden Temple with his family two days after Blue Star had ended. He was broken after seeing what the Indian Government had done.

It was October 31st, 1984, when Gandhi was walking towards the interview room in her complex. With her, walked three other bodyguards and the keeping guard at the wicket gate was her favorite bodyguard; Beant Singh. As she entered, she saw Beant Singh and his fellow companion, Satwant Singh. Satwant Singh that morning had requested a change in his posting, he wanted to be with Beant.

Upon Indira's entrance, at 9:29 am, both Singhs emptied their rifles on the former president. After throwing down his weapon, Beant Singh was shot on the spot while Satwant was taken into custody.

Indira was rushed to the A.I.I.M.S hospital in New Delhi. Ten hours after her death, all Indian radio listeners found out that Gandhi had died in the hospital and her two assassinators were Sikh men. A large quantity of Hindus formed a huge crowd in front of the hospital. To them, now every Sikh seemed like an assassin. They had just killed their mother.

There were people traveling all over India on trains and for several journeys, the mid-way stop was the train station that lay outside of Delhi. When trains approached, the outraged group of Hindu citizens barged in and shouted 'Grab them, Grab them. They killed our mother!".

They pulled out any man who was wearing a turban and took all his possessions. Then they were taken onto the platform and burned down.

Evening fell and many Sikhs that were in Delhi went into other peoples' homes that were not Sikh and hid there. If they had stayed on their own, they would've lost their lives. The others that were on the streets were burned down, shot, and sliced in front of their families. The police had told the Sikhs to go somewhere safe and if they did that then they would protect them otherwise they would get killed. 50,000 people had fled Delhi and 3000 deaths had been reported in that city alone. Temples were set on fire and homes were destroyed. Lives were changing.

After a couple of days, things had settled down.

Fast forward to March 1986, the Golden Temple complex had been taken over once again. The military again planned a solution named Operation Black Thunder to expel the 200 militants.

Around 1000 guards and border security barged in and captured the militants. While no extreme resistance was reported, there was one death.

The second part of this operation, sometimes referred to as 'Operation Black Thunder II' took place from May 8th to the 19th. Its purpose was to expel militants from the Golden Temple complex. This operation was far more effective because all the militants surrendered in peace with zero casualties. News journalists were allowed full access inside the complex upon the ending and Kirtan resumed in the Temple shortly.

There was a huge difference between Operation Blue Star and Operation Black Thunder. Yes, the people on both sides were different as well but looking back at the impacts of Operation Blue Star, the militants and military had understood the implications of such actions.

There is a lot to learn from this. In the end, we can all agree that everyone has their own ways and opinions about how to live. Intentions can be honest, but the demand can be executed poorly. Indians believe that these events happened because God wants them to and it's all written in one's destiny. In other minds what is predictable is preventable. Therefore, till today Jarnail Singh and Gandhi's deaths are destiny to some while to others murder.

Even today many families haven't been able to forget this dreadful event. Times have changed with changed relationships and mentalities. We live in a whole new generation where Hindus and Sikhs are bonded; some are friends while others are even relatives. The event of Diwali also known as the event of lights or good over evil is celebrated by both cultures together.

There are however today some people who still want Khalistan. Maybe it's not about the state, it's more of an independent identity. Some people still exist who seek revenge on Kuldip and are content with Indira's assassination. It would be to everyone's benefit if we all created peace; Bhindranwale was an inspiration for a lot of people and will be forever. At one point creating peace between all was his intention. Even though he isn't in this world his words still echo in some people's ears, "Khalistan Raaj Karega' (Khalistan will rule). There is no right or wrong side to this. We are all entitled to say, do and believe in whatever we wish to, whether that is influenced by our upbringing or own mindsets, as long as others are not being hurt.

Bhindranwale might have started with a pure vision but it seemed throughout his journey he was pushed onto the wrong track where he started taking the direction of violence to get what he wanted. That was not what our Guru's inspired us to do, in fact, we were taught the opposite.

However, maybe Bhindranwale and others were frustrated because no one had listened to the Sikhs raise their voices for so many years. The British emerged as Punjab to be a part of India before their departure, not realizing what they had done to the independent identity of Sikhs and their religion.

The other side of the story tells us how unfair the government and justice system were and is in India. The rules change for political figures but are a hundred times harder on someone with no power. It shows us, one of the best leaders in the world, possessed no quality of being culturally competent.

Indira Gandhi failed to recognize the impact of sending the military and tanks into the temple as it destroyed not only the physical building but also the sentiments of Sikhs. The Sikh community had honored Guru Arjan Dev Ji and the curfew had been reinforced in no time. The marble steps were destroyed, and the military had entered the complex with shoes.

When this situation is examined, politics and religion do not tend to work well cohesively, which was the main belief of the Shiromani Akali Dal. Politics and religion share different mindsets because one involves ideologies and actions from the heart and soul while the other involves the manipulation of people, sometimes even against each other.

That may not be relevant in all countries, but the Indian political system has seen its fair share of discrimination and corruption throughout the years. Unethical practices like these are so deeply rooted in the system, that even if we tried to fix it, we would fail before we even started.

PART THREE

THE LAST CALL: AIR INDIA 182

Inderjit Singh Reyat was a family man living happily with his wife and three children in a quiet neighborhood in Surrey, British Columbia, Canada. Punjab's unsettling environment in January 1984 forced him to move out west. He had seen Punjab's situation deteriorating and had followed what other families were doing. Moving away.

He was your typical man that had seen Canada as an opportunity to provide himself and his family with a better and secure future. A future that didn't involve violence or the uncertainty of even waking up the next morning.

He had a car garage that he worked at five days a week and spent most of his weekends with his family and doing selfless service at the local Gurudwara. He had built quite the rapport with the regular attendees of the Gurudwara and many knew him as an outgoing and straightforward man.

Talwinder Singh Parmar was a close friend of Reyat. They had met not too long ago, but it had seemed like they had known each other for ages. Parmar was the head of the organization: Babbar Khalsa, whose main objective was to create an independent nation in the name of Khalistan. Though they were based in Vancouver, their reach stretched to countries in Europe as well.

Many individuals from the community and around the world supported this and even followed and preached to Parmar. Reyat had become good friends with Parmar shortly after his arrival due to their similar ways of thinking.

In fact, there were several individuals who shared the same dedication towards the religion and had formed an alliance with one another at the local Gurudwara. They all identified themselves as part of the Babbar Khalsa and wanted to continue the legacy Bhindranwale had started not so long ago.

After Bhindranwale's death, there was a large outcry not only in India but internationally as well which got worse after October 1984. The Babbar Khalsa had claimed at their gatherings, "Blood for blood and...we will not rest until fifty thousand Hindus die."

A very concerning statement. It could have been just out of frustration, but what happened in the months to come would say otherwise.

As these gatherings happened in the local Gurudwara, there were many instances where members of the Babbar Khalsa would preach in front of their community and make such statements. One day, Ajaib Singh Bagri said seven words that would then initiate a criminal investigation against them.

It was obvious, the Babbar Khalsa wanted to revenge on Indian Government for what they had done.

Ajaib Singh Bagri had said in one of the gatherings that "Planes will fall out of the sky." The statement was directed more towards the flag carrier of India, Air India. The objective was to tarnish the reputation of the country but do it on an international level. The Royal Canadian Mounted Police started their investigation after this threatening statement had caught their attention.

The investigation involved the first suspect, Talwinder Singh Parmar, who was under surveillance 24/7 because of his alliances and involvement in the Babbar Khalsa.

A stakeout was carried out in front of Parmar's residence to determine any clues that could indicate a planned attack. Investigators kept track of where he went, what he purchased, who he met, and who came to his residence. It felt to the investigators that Parmar had an idea of what was going on, which was why he was very cautious in his day-to-day life. He only stepped out to visit his local Gurudwara to pray in the mornings or the local market to buy his weekly essentials. He did however have people come to visit him at his residence more often. There was increased activity in his calls, which pushed the investigators to tap his calls.

Many phone calls on a daily basis were tapped, however since they were in Punjabi, it was difficult for the investigators to understand their language. They had to send the recordings to Ottawa, Ontario, for translation. During these exchanges, it had been determined that one of the frequently called contacts of Parmar was Inderjit Singh Reyat. This initiated an investigation into Reyat as well.

This activity continued for about two months and it was noted that these phone calls had become less frequent. One Saturday, Reyat had skipped going to the Gurudwara and was witnessed in Vancouver Island. Since investigators had received this news after his visit, it was unknown what his purpose for the visit was. However, this did not stop officers from going to Vancouver Island to investigate his visit.

After a long tiring search, officers ended up in a small shop located in Duncan. The owner had recalled seeing Inderjit just the day before as he had made a large purchase. His receipts showed a purchase of a SANYO radio and some clocks.

While these investigators were in Duncan, another set of officers followed Parmar and Reyat that day, who were in another part of Vancouver Island. It was observed that the men had walked into a forest with a black bag together.

To not get caught, the investigators had stood farther from the men which resulted in them not being able to have a visual but they could hear them conversing in their language. As this conversation was happening, suddenly, a loud noise disrupted the first. Birds flew out of their nests and there were a couple of seconds of this chaos and confusion on the investigator's faces. Had a riffle just gone off? A bomb? Had one of them killed the other?

As the officers are trying to figure this out, Reyat and Parmar are seen walking out of the forest back to their vehicles. At this time, the other set of officers in Duncan communicate to the ones in the forest about Inderjit's purchase of the radio and clocks - which confirmed their suspicion that a bomb had gone off in the forest.

Through their findings, a couple of days later the investigators ended up at a construction sight where they learned Reyat had visited a few days ago and had asked to 'test' a machine they were making. Reyat had told the workers a false narrative that he was from a construction company himself and had designed something in regard to the work and wanted to test it in that setting.

The manager had let Reyat carry out this test as they believed him. Reyat had planted this black bag on the far side of the construction site and stood beside the workers. He then continued to 'show' them how the machine worked. He pressed a button, an explosion happened and he explained how his machine would be beneficial and easier for construction demolition.

Before the workers could ask him more questions, Reyat got into his car and drove away saying he would be back later.

THE LAST CALL: AIR INDIA 182

A couple of days later, news that Rajiv Gandhi was visiting the United States was circulating. After Indira's death, Rajiv was sworn in as the Prime Minister and had been taking care of political duties since November 1984. Could this be the possible flight that would be bombed?

As the investigators monitored this flight, they were relieved to find out Rajiv's flight hadn't seen any terrorist activity when he visited on June 19, 1985. At this point, investigators had doubts that if those words said by Ajaib Singh were an empty threat or if something was really going to really happen.

On June 21, investigators intercepted a 30-second phone call between Reyat and Parmar. The conversation seemed very unusual:

Parmar: "Have you wrote the book yet?"
Reyat: "No, not yet"
Parmar: "Write it right away."

Amidst this terrorism-related investigation, there was a conversation about writing a book. Officers were quick to denote that it had to be some sort of code for what was really about to happen.

It's early morning on June 23rd, 1985 at Vancouver International Airport. CP is getting a flight ready for Toronto that departs just in a few hours. Most passengers would be connected to Air India 182 from this CP flight once they land at Pearson Airport, Toronto.

People are lined up in long queues, waiting to check in their baggage with CP Air and amongst these people stands Inderjit Singh Reyat with his passport and black bag. His flight ticket reads the name, *M. Singh*.

"Sir, your baggage is only checked in for Toronto. You'll have to pick up your back and re-check into Air India at Pearson."

The CP Air ticket attendant realized Reyat's bag was only going to Toronto and not the rest of the journey. Reyat did not seem happy about this which led him to raise his voice and speak in a threatening tone.

His voice could be heard throughout the hall and people had shifted their attention toward the ticket counter. The ticket attendant felt sweat running down her back and could feel her face turning red.

"Okay, sir! I'll check it in but you'll have to confirm with Air India once you land in Delhi."

After calming down, Reyat made his way toward the exit instead of security. He gets off the escalators and is about to continue his walk when someone shouts his name. He turns around.

It's his friend, a community member he's seen several times at the Gurudwara. The friend gets into a conversation as he's dropping off his family and questions Reyat about his presence at the airport.

Reyat, brushing off those questions, tells his friend he's running late and must leave at once. The friend was stuck wondering why Inderjit was there alone without any baggage but realized he could be dropping off someone.

The bags are boarded, and the passengers on CP Air are on their way to Toronto. Once in Toronto, the passengers and baggage are now shifted onto a Boeing 737 that would be flying as Air India 182. In addition to the passengers connecting from CP Air, new passengers join them from Toronto.

The atmosphere is totally different at Pearson. A passenger dropped off his wife and daughter that day and as he's checking

THE LAST CALL: AIR INDIA 182

in at Air India, he looks over at British Airways check-in. All the passengers are Sikh, turbaned men. Not a single individual of that appearance was seen on Air India's side.

During the past year, the Babbar Khalsa had made it clear in their gatherings that all Sikhs had to boycott Air India. During this time British Airways saw a dramatic increase in sales as their Toronto-London-Delhi route had become popular.

329 passengers and crew were all set to fly that afternoon. The flight took off without any disturbances.

About 6 hours later, Air India 182 makes its last radio call with Irish Air Traffic controller, Michael Quinn and disappears off of the radar. Passengers would have been waking up and breakfast would have been served shortly. That never happens. An explosive decompression caused by the bomb ends the lives of all passengers in seconds.

The bomb going off in mid-air caused the fuselage of the aircraft to break into several pieces before hitting the water, and the impact of the bomb killed most passengers in mid-air. There couldn't be any survivors.

Another small impact bomb moments prior goes off at a terminal in Narita International Airport, Japan. There were five injured and 2 dead but the link? The flight had started its journey in Vancouver and was traveling to India.

The next several months are spent by the aviation industry and RCMP investigating the accident.

The aviation industry changed a lot of its standards and practices after this devastating event. Passengers not present on the flight with checked-in baggage would have their baggage removed from the aircraft. If Reyat's bag had been removed, there was a higher chance of this not occurring.

Checking in bags properly was another area that was looked at. Ticket attendants were trained to deal with difficult passengers and only perform check-ins according to what they had been informed. If Reyat's bag had only been checked-in for Toronto, it would have gone through security once again and it would have been caught.

On that June 23rd morning, the x-ray machines for baggage inspection had stopped working in Vancouver. Security had to use hand-held explosive testing devices to determine if there were any explosives in bags. When Reyat's bag was inspected, the machine went off - but the bag was let through as the sound was rather different. It's a bit hard to believe that the x-ray machines had stopped performing on the day of this flight in specific and that Reyat's bag was let through. Though there's no evidence, suspicions arose that someone from the airport had been involved in this crime. Therefore, advanced security systems would need to be developed to detect explosives and other hazards.

Aviation experts started developing materials and mechanisms that could be used to protect not only the black and red boxes but also the fuselage of the aircraft. Options were explored for more durable materials to build planes with so that explosive decompressions would have a lesser effect and pilots could have time to get to safety without the aircraft falling apart mid-flight.

As the trial unfolded in the next several months in Vancouver's courtrooms, the crime and its criminals had finally come to light. Talwinder Singh fled to India in 1990, right before these trials began but was encountered by Punjab Police and pronounced dead on scene.

THE LAST CALL: AIR INDIA 182

The story of this heartless crime involved Hardial Singh Johal, who worked as a janitor in a local elementary school. He was seen at the airport on the day Reyat dropped off his bag, potentially could have been the one to check in the other bag that exploded in Narita too. His phone number was left behind with the ticket agent he booked tickets with. Some suspicions about this individual included that he had hidden the bomb in the basement of the school he worked at while it was under construction. There was no hard evidence found against Johal, which is why he was acquitted.

Investigators then had Inderjit Singh Reyat arrested for manslaughter with the evidence they possessed. The interrogation that occurred before the court appearance was quite a movie. At first, Reyat had denied all the evidence against him and claimed he knew nothing about these events. He knew the officers weren't going to let him go this easily and he had a family at home. He finally gave in after several hours. He admitted to having a hand in constructing both bombs but refused to reveal any information about the others that were involved.

Later on, Hardial Singh Johal passed away in 2003 due to a heart attack and in the same year Inderjit Singh Reyat, a Canadian national, was the only individual convicted for blowing up Air India 182. He was sentenced to 18 years in prison for manslaughter but that sentence was shortened to 15. Was justice really served?

It was a legacy started by one man in 1984 that was set out to change people for the better, but did that really happen? It was a sequence of events that unfolded one after the other that caused the death of 329 innocent people and many more in the state of Punjab the previous year. In the demand for basic rights, Bhindranwale's vision steered off track and ideologies became lost in translation. Using violence was never encouraged or supported by the Sikh Gurus, so how were these individuals doing such actions in the name of religion?

Since the violence in India had started, up until the Air India bombing, someone lost their wife, daughter, son, brother, best friend and so much more. Not only that, Sikhs had to deal with racism and discrimination in the coming years all over the world.

One Sikh individual who had flown to Ireland to identify his wife's body recalled how others were claiming "You guys did it." It's the equivalent of what Muslims have to hear due to Al Quead's actions.

These groups of misguided individuals mask their wrongdoings in the name of religion, which is borderline inhumane. The Babbar Khalsa's goal was to help people, teach them about the heroic deeds and sacrifices our Gurus made, and not resort to violence and take innocent lives. Yes, you're trying to revenge on the Indian Government for their destruction of the Golden Temple. Yes, the government killed innocent people - but what makes you different then? The world is aware there are several government systems so corrupt that you can never fix them. So what's the solution? Do you become them?

You cannot label a whole race as a terrorist because a few lost individuals decided to make an inhumane decision that day. You cannot generalize people into a category and assume all are like that. These topics can be sensitive and triggering, but the truth always hurts.

Reflecting back to what Lt. Kuldip Singh Brar said about Bhindranwale, "he was a misguided man who needed to be

THE LAST CALL: AIR INDIA 182

brought back", connects greatly to all the individuals involved in Air India 182, and even others who have been a part of terrorist activity. If you think violence is going to change the world, why did world wars occur? They didn't solve anything but create resentment between countries and build fear and hatred in people.

The bombing changed the way people looked at air travel and for the coming years there was a slight decrease in air travel to certain Asian locations. The economy for tourism also saw a slight decrease in its revenue due to these external threats. Airport security was vigilantly trained to check baggage items and what people carried with them. Screenings upon entering countries became more intense and any flagged passengers were to be investigated rigorously.

We continue to battle with differentiating worldviews and cognitive patterns because everyone grows up with different beliefs. We are living with different values, and attitudes that may or may not be responsible for our actions and reactions on such sensitive issues but violence should never be the answer.

It was a back-and-forth response that involved first Operation Blue Star, Indira's assassination, and then Air India 182. The people involved were making innocent people pay the price for their disagreements with the government and vice versa.

Education and being aware of how cultures and religions function differently around the world is the most important quality a leader needs to have, which clearly Indira Gandhi and office didn't have. Overall, understanding that violence is not the answer to our problems will help make our planet a more livable place. Is that going to happen? No. Can we try? Yes.

Why won't it happen? There's always going to be that one person, or that one government system that is going to try again and again to break people apart - because it benefits them.

Apparently, it's become a norm in today's world even though most us try to stay far from such things.

As stated before, this topic was a sensitive one with no black-and-white sides. It has a lot of gray areas and so many opinions form with the influence of personal experiences and perspectives. Some individuals may be triggered by opinions presented here, however, we must ask ourselves why are we triggered. It's a known fact that both sides of this situation were to blame for the way they reacted, yet we try to justify each side with reasoning to make it sound like it was not their fault. It has been noted that certain views are unvalidated by making things about religion, when they're not.

After all this, it should be evident how important education is to understand such issues and react in the appropriate manner. It can be seen so many times in history, one being recent.

The 2020 Indian Farmer Protests is a prime example.

The protests broke out because there was a change in rules for harvest selling. The old business model suggested farmers take their harvest to the market and sell through a vendor. They would get their earnings within a month minus the vendor fees at the maximum selling price. The new business model suggests that you can sell your harvest for a price you decide on. Any businesses wanting to buy products from farmers will approach them without the vendors being involved and the farmers would get paid within 48 hours. The second part of the new business model was that farmers were now allowed to rent their land to people for four times the price.

THE LAST CALL: AIR INDIA 182

In theory, this would have been the ideal practice as it would provide more independent freedom to the farmers to do business on their own terms. It took maybe one piece of misinformation to spread among everyone which resulted in this outcry that the Indian Government was taking away their rights. This is what essentially caused the protests.

Yes, people will be upset, and triggered and would want to defend themselves by presenting information that had zero credibility and call others liars or traitors because they don't support this movement. but that's the point. They're not educated enough to understand what these new rules are about. They're not to blame, it is the system that doesn't allow for such growth for the citizens and the lack of availability or resources adds a new problem.

There have been countless baseless arguments on how the Indian government is unfair to the farmers, however, did anyone take a moment to understand the new laws and their impacts or did they just follow everyone else and join the crowd? It's easy to join this crowd, but much more difficult to actually understand and weigh an issue and then stand up for what's right.

Those who did understand and tried to speak about it were told to keep their mouth shut and not talk about this issue. Out of nowhere religion comes into play and then the people start comparing that. It's appalling how religion all of a sudden comes into play with political issues even when it's not instigated. Why do people have a hard time understanding that political actions are meant to be performed against people, not religions?

If facts want to be explored, then people must understand there were meetings with the government during these protests, the bills were revoked and farmers were given an option to pick the new or old business model. The issue lies in people not analyzing facts and just reacting based off of what others tell them. There's no credibility or even an attempt to verify information and let's also not forget that everything was turned into being about religion for some reason.

If only the education system was more accessible and feasible to all, it would prevent such misunderstandings to happen. Education would allow citizens to have a better understanding of laws such as these and give them the ability to make educated decisions. They would be able to fight for their rights using the law system and pass this down to the next generation.

That's the one example that should illustrate clearly why education, cultural competence, and understanding different views are vital while we are living together.

Of course, you cannot convince everyone to follow or think the same way, but we can make room for all opinions to exist and have respect for each other, whether we agree or not.

THE END

OTHER TITLES BY AMANAT GILL

A Few Secrets

Amanat Gill
September 2020

Thorns and Roses

Amanat Gill
December 2023

THE LAST CALL: AIR INDIA 182

Available on Amazon worldwide

www.ingramcontent.com/pod-product-compliance
Ingram Content Group UK Ltd.
Pitfield, Milton Keynes, MK11 3LW, UK
UKHW022211230426
12048UKWH00016BA/776